THE FOUNDING OF THE AFL

AND THE RISE OF ORGANIZED LABOR

WEST BEND COMMUNITY MEMORIAL LIBRARY

THE FOUNDING OF THE AFL

AND THE RISE OF ORGANIZED LABOR

Patricia Simonds

Silver Burdett Press

Acknowledgments
The author and editor thank the following people for their invaluable help in text and picture research: Tina Angelos; Lynda DeLoache, George Meany Memorial Archives; and Thomas Featherstone, Archives of Labor and Urban Affairs, Wayne State University.

Consultants
We thank the following people for reviewing the manuscript and offering their helpful suggestions:

Robert M. Goldberg
Consultant to the Social Studies Department (formerly
  Department Chair)
Oceanside Middle School
Oceanside, New York

Karen E. Markoe
Professor of History
Maritime College of the State
  University of New York

Cover: *This poster from the early 1900s is titled* The Bone and Sinew of America. *Courtesy of the Archives Center, National Museum of American History. Not to be reproduced without the express written permission of the Smithsonian Institution.*

Title Page: *The Knights of Labor parade in New York City at the first Labor Day celebration, September 5, 1882. The Granger Collection.*

Contents Page: *A pro-labor engraving from the 1880s. Archives of Labor and Urban Affairs, Wayne State University.*

Back Cover: *Samuel Gompers, founder of the AFL. The Granger Collection.*

Library of Congress Cataloging-in-Publication Data

Simonds, Patricia.
    The founding of the AFL and the rise of organized labor / Patricia
  Simonds.
        p.   cm. -- (Turning Points in American history)
    Includes bibliographical references and index.
        Summary: Recounts the story of the American Federation of Labor
  and other early unions in their efforts to organize labor for the
  struggle to secure better wages and working conditions, and shorter
  workdays.
        1. American Federation of Labor--History--Juvenile literature.
  2. Trade-unions--United States--History--Juvenile literature.
    [1. American Federation of Labor--History. 2. Labor movement.]
    I. Title. II. Series.
      HD8055.A5S56 1991
      331. 88 ' 32' 0973--dc20

91-10556
CIP
AC

Editorial Coordination by Richard G. Gallin

 Created by Media Projects Incorporated

Carter Smith, *Executive Editor*
Charles A. Wills, *Series Editor*
Bernard Schleifer, *Design Consultant*
Arlene Goldberg, *Cartographer*

Copyright © 1991 by Silver Burdett Press, Inc., a division of Simon & Schuster, Englewood Cliffs, New Jersey.

All rights reserved, including the right of reproduction in whole or part in any form.

Manufactured in the United States of America.

ISBN 0-382-24123-1 [lib. bdg.]
10 9 8 7 6 5 4 3 2 1

ISBN 0-382-24118-5 [pbk.]
10 9 8 7 6 5 4 3 2 1

J
331.88
Si5

CONTENTS

INTRODUCTION

SAMUEL GOMPERS'S DREAM

On December 8, 1886, forty-two delegates from twenty-five labor organizations met in Columbus, Ohio. They met to discuss their differences with what was then the largest organization representing American workers—the Knights of Labor.

The delegates were all from trade unions. (Unions are groups of workers engaged in the same kind of work who band together to win better treatment from their employers.) They wanted some independence within the Knights, but the discussions came to nothing. The Knights' leadership refused to listen.

In response, the delegates at Columbus decided to set up their own organization and restrict it to trade unions alone. Thus the American Federation of Labor, soon known as the AFL, was born.

The delegates elected Samuel Gompers, an official of the Cigar Makers

This AFL marching banner was carried in parades and rallies.

Union, as president. He was to "devote his entire time to … the Federation."

Gompers later wrote: "I was in my young manhood. I had devoted myself to the cause of labor and the people, and it was my earnest purpose to give all that was in me in that cause."

The presidency of the AFL was Sam Gompers's first paid position in the labor movement but not his first experience with labor unions.

Born in London of Dutch parents in 1850, he came to New York City with his parents in 1863. Sam and his father found work as cigarmakers. They soon joined the cigarmakers' union, and young Gompers found a job in a union shop—a workplace that hires only members of a certain union—in 1873.

The other workers in the shop were an interesting group. Most were from Europe. They talked all day about politics and labor unions. Everyone chipped in to pay one of their group to read aloud as they worked. In this way, young Sam Gompers learned about the ideas of Karl

Strikers for an eight-hour day threaten nonstriking workers in New York, 1874.

Marx, Charles Fourier, and other European socialists. (Socialism is the belief that the government should own and run most industries.)

One of Sam Gompers's co-workers was a Swede, Karl Laurrell, a union man through and through. He had been secretary of the section of the International Workingman's Association (an early international labor union) that covered Denmark, Norway, and Sweden. Laurrell was familiar with theories about improving the conditions of working people, and he became Gompers's mentor.

Young Gompers once went to Laurrell for advice. He never forgot what he heard. Laurrell told him, "Study your union card, Sam, and if the idea doesn't come square with that, it ain't true."

In 1873, a depression struck business activity in the United States. Companies made less money than before, and some failed and shut down. Workers were laid off, and those who managed to keep their jobs had to accept lower wages. Many of those who lost their jobs also lost their homes because they couldn't pay rent.

Hunger became a problem among the unemployed. Politicians did little to help working people.

Gompers wrote later that "Christmas in New York was not festive that year." Unions and other organizations tried to help, but they couldn't do much. To win support for their cause, unions published pamphlets and staged protest demonstrations. These frightened the better-off classes. The atmosphere in New York City was full of discontent and distrust.

To build support for the working people, a public rally was planned for January 13, 1874. Newspapers and politicians called the organizers "radicals," but in fact they were only American imitators of European socialists. Gompers had no part in organizing the event, but he wanted to attend.

He arrived early at Tompkins Square that day. The walled-in park quickly filled with people. At about 10:30 A.M., policemen surrounded the area.

Shortly afterward a large group carrying the sign Tenth Ward Union Labor marched up. The police moved swiftly to break up the parade, hurting bystanders in the process. Gompers escaped injury by jumping into a cellar doorway.

Gompers had learned a lesson. As he later wrote: "I saw that leadership in the labor movementcould be safely entrusted only to those into whose hearts and minds had been woven the experiences of earning their daily bread by labor."

Not for Sam Gompers were the idealists and theorists. They wrote fine pamphlets and drew big crowds to their rallies, but few of them had dirtied their hands with honest labor.

Gompers knew what he wanted: a better deal for American working people. A century after the American Revolution and twenty years after Abraham Lincoln freed the slaves, many U.S. workers were still being denied basic rights.

If a single worker was being paid too little, or forced to work too many hours of the day, there was little he or she could do. But if all workers in a factory—or even better, all the workers in one industry—acted together, they had power to improve their lives. This is what Samuel Gompers believed when he became the first president of the AFL. The new organization encouraged and helped the formation and growth of unions in various trades. The AFL sought to raise wages for workers, to improve conditions in the workplace, and to limit working hours. Unlike some other labor organizations, the AFL under Samuel Gompers worked to accomplish these peacefully, through cooperation and negotiation.

By 1901, the AFL's membership had climbed almost to the million mark.

THE FEDERATION OF LABOR

TRADES UNIONISTS FORM A NEW ORGANIZATION.

THE KNIGHTS OF LABOR IGNORED AND A CONSTITUTION FOR THE NEW BODY ADOPTED—OFFICERS ELECTED.

COLUMBUS, Ohio, Dec. 11.—It will doubtless prove a trifle galling to Terence Vincent Powderly and his old Executive Board to learn that the trades unionists, who have been in session here for the best part of a week, have elected as President of their new organization, the American Federation of Labor, Samuel Gompers, the man he so vilified in the "secret" circular that was printed in to-day's TIMES. The fact that Mr. Gompers was elected without opposition may give Mr. Powderly an idea of the estimation in which he is held by trades unionists. The latter are now prepared to go their own way. They did not invite interference or opposition, in the first place, and if Mr. Powderly's lieutenants with his knowledge had not abused their powers so grossly there would be peace to-day between organizations that are now rivals. The new organization has no fear of the Knights, for its membership was in existence long before they were thought of. It begins life with 25 trades unions as a nucleus. There is reason to suppose that as many more will join the fold before another convention is held. Its primary object is to secure as members every trade and labor union in the country, and some of the steps it has taken to attain this object show the shrewdness of the builders.

Heretofore the Knights have been enabled to enroll all the workers in small communities. A glance at the Federation's constitution will show that such a field will no longer be left exclusively to the "noble order." The Knights have been enabled to secure many members by a promise of general assistance in case of a strike or lockout. Such assistance has proved by experience but a broken reed. The Federation's constitution provides that, under certain circumstances, assistance of a general character will be given in case of strikes or lockouts, and unionists know that their treasuries are seldom empty, and that among them a promise has usually amounted to fulfillment. Then members of the Federation will be allowed self-government. As among the Knights, a cigarmaker will not, among trades unions, be allowed to march into a silk mill and order a strike. The leaders of the new movement are tried men. The work is not new to them. They are acquainted with the weak spots in the "noble order" as well as in trades unions, and they have labored hard to construct such an organization that will not need constant tinkering. They think they have succeeded, and they talk like men who have satisfactorily accomplished a difficult task, upon adjournment late this afternoon.

This newspaper article describes the AFL's founding in December 1886.

THE TRIAL

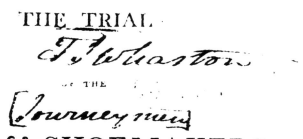

J. Wharton

OF THE

[Journeymen]

BOOT & SHOEMAKERS

OF PHILADELPHIA,

ON AN INDICTMENT

FOR A COMBINATION AND CONSPIRACY

TO RAISE THEIR WAGES.

TAKEN IN SHORT-HAND,
BY THOMAS LLOYD.

PHILADELPHIA:

PRINTED BY B. GRAVES, NO. 40, NORTH FOURTH-STREET,
FOR T. LLOYD, AND B. GRAVES.

....
1806.

1

LABOR IN THE NINETEENTH CENTURY

The United States began as a land of farms and small towns. In the year 1800, there were only five large cities—Boston, New York, Philadelphia, Baltimore, and Charleston. Only a few thousand people lived in cities—not the millions who do so today.

The coming of the Industrial Revolution changed the face of the United States. New towns grew up around the factories because factory workers needed to be housed, fed, clothed, and entertained. As business and industry expanded, the cities grew also. The promise of earning a better living and having a better life drew more and more workers to the factories.

Workers changed, too. No longer did a person have to possess a particular skill to be employed. The coming of machines meant that a worker needed to know only enough to keep a machine running.

Workers who tried to organize unions were often charged with "conspiracy," as this title page to an account of an 1806 strike shows.

Because skill wasn't a requirement for work in the new mills and factories, children were employed, too. In the early nineteenth century, half of all factory workers were children of nine or ten years—or even younger. These children worked the same hours as adults but for less pay.

The Industrial Revolution changed the way Americans lived and worked. But the new and more complicated economy of the country often stumbled.

Every few years, money became scarce. Banks didn't have as much money to lend to business, and prices for factory products fell. During these "slumps," factory owners lengthened the hours of work, cut workers' pay, and often fired "unneeded" workers. Some businesses failed, and whole families—men, women, and children—lost their jobs. By the early 1840s, after an especially bad business period, the United States had its first large group of unemployed citizens. These people had no one to help them and nowhere to turn. Labor unions as we know them today didn't exist then.

Working conditions varied from one industry to another. What almost all workers had in common were long hours (twelve, thirteen, even fourteen or more hours per day, six days a week—sometimes seven), low wages, and no assurance they would keep their jobs.

Early mills and factories weren't healthful or safe. Textile mills had huge turning gears that could easily catch and rip off a finger. In iron foundries, according to a writer of the era, people worked "bent to the ground... over boiling cauldrons of metal" giving off unhealthy fumes into "air saturated with fog and grease and soot."

Many employers showed little concern for the conditions their workers labored in. One mill owner actually said, "I regard my work people just as I regard my machinery."

There had been early attempts to set up unions. As early as 1778, printers in New York City organized a successful strike. (In a strike, workers refuse to work until their demands are met.) In the 1790s, Philadelphia shoemakers started a union. But these were skilled craftsmen. Each union was organized according to the trade of its members. In the early 1800s, carpenters, mechanics, barrel makers (then called coopers), furniture makers, and masons banded together. They bargained with their employers for better working conditions, for more pay, and to protect their jobs.

In Lowell, Massachusetts, in 1844,

Sara G. Bagley organized the Female Labor Reform Association. This was a new sort of group. Its members had different skills, but they all worked in the same industry, tending the machines that made raw cotton into cloth. From its original five members in Lowell, the association grew to more than six hundred in several different cities within a year.

The biggest goal of the association and the trade unions of skilled workers was a ten-hour working day. Twelve to fourteen hours of work a day was too long, they insisted. The groups asked Congress and state legislatures to limit working hours, but progress was slow. It was not until 1840 that President Martin Van Buren made the first move and set a ten-hour day for those who worked for the federal government. States gradually followed the federal example: New Hampshire in 1847 and then Connecticut, Maine, Rhode Island, Ohio, and Georgia. But the laws could be easily gotten around. A "special contract" could be written requiring longer working hours. If workers didn't sign this contract, they didn't get the job. And these laws usually applied only to workers with government jobs, so they offered no protection to the great majority of workers in private businesses.

Adding to the problems of working people was the increasing number of new immigrants from other nations. The failure of the potato crop in Ireland and political upheavals in Europe caused many people to cross the Atlantic Ocean looking for a new home and way of life in the United States. Between 1846 and 1855,

In this cartoon, Britain unsuccessfully tries to stop its citizens from emigrating to America.

more than 3 million immigrants came to the United States—three times more than in all the previous fifty years.

This flood of people created a huge supply of labor. Some employers didn't feel they had to pay attention to their workers' needs. If workers didn't like the hours they worked or the wages they were paid, they could easily be replaced by immigrant labor. Immigrants, glad to have any job, were not likely to cause trouble, the factory owners thought.

Trade unions as we know them today began to take shape in the 1850s. Local union groups began to band together nationally. There had been groups of plumbers, carpenters, hatmakers, and so forth in individual cities for many years. Now the idea began to spread that they would be more powerful if all the workers in a trade banded together for common goals.

The leader and guiding spirit of this movement was William H. Sylvis. Sylvis was an iron molder (a worker who pours molten iron into molds to produce metal goods, like tools and pots) from Pennsylvania. He learned the skills of his trade from local ironworks, later finding work in Philadelphia. He joined the two-year-old Philadelphia Iron Molders Union in 1857. When the factory Sylvis worked in

William H. Sylvis.

cut wages, he was one of the first to walk out on strike. This was the beginning of what was to become his life's work: organizing unions.

As its secretary, Sylvis put in long hours working for the union—after he finished working at the factory. He kept in touch with other groups of iron molders around the country. Late in 1858, he called for a meeting in Philadelphia on July 4, 1859. Forty-six iron molders from eighteen cities came. They voted to establish the National Molders Union. The group wasn't united in its aims until 1863, when Sylvis was elected president of the union. From then on he never stopped working to strengthen the union.

Sylvis traveled all over the United States and Canada. In his first year as head of the union, he traveled 10,000 miles. He built membership in the union with hardly any money. Sometimes he begged rides in the cabs of locomotives because he didn't have train fare. When he couldn't afford a hotel, he stayed in the homes of union members.

His brother reported about these trips: "He wore clothes until they became quite threadbare and he could wear them no longer. The shawl he wore to the day of his death... was filled with little holes burned there by the splashing of molten iron from the ladles of molders in strange cities, whom he was beseeching to organize."

Everywhere he went, he talked about the benefits of joining the union. By the time of the National Molders Union's national convention in 1864, Sylvis could report that membership in the union had grown from 2,000 to 3,500. But he didn't stop working. He traveled tirelessly, recruiting members and getting local chapters organized and admitted to the national group. By 1867, the union, now called the Iron Molders International Union, because it had members in Canada, had 9,000 members.

During his years as president, Sylvis began many procedures that unions continue to follow today. Control lay with the national organization, and only it could call strikes. Each member had to contribute money to a fund used to help support members during a strike. A union newspaper was published to inform and educate the members.

Sylvis was also a leader in the movement for an eight-hour day. In 1868, he and other union leaders urged President Andrew Johnson to support the idea. In June of that year, Congress established eight hours as the legal working day for federal employees.

Sylvis became increasingly interested in the political strength of national labor unions—not just the Iron Molders. In 1868, he was elected president of the National Labor Union at a meeting attended by trade unionists, antibusiness groups, and two fighters for women's rights, Susan B. Anthony and Elizabeth Cady Stanton. Under his leadership, the National Labor Union tried to unite such groups as farmers, women's rights leaders, freed slaves, and trade unionists into a powerful new organization.

The National Labor Union was not a labor union as we know them today. It was more interested in achieving political goals than improving working conditions. William Sylvis died in 1869, before the National Labor Union's next convention. Without his leadership, it tried to pursue too many goals. Within three years of Sylvis's death, the National Labor Union disappeared.

LEADERS OF THE KNIGHTS OF LABOR.

COPYRIGHTED 1886 BY KURZ & ALLISON, ART PUBLISHERS, 76 & 78 WABASH AVE, CHICAGO, U.S.A.

2

THE KNIGHTS OF LABOR

Some thought the idea of organizing laborers would fade away after William Sylvis' death. But just five years later, in December 1869, nine tailors in Philadelphia founded a new organization to promote better conditions—including higher wages and a shorter workday—for American workers. After a few weeks they added six new members.

The new group was a secret society so that employers couldn't punish members. The name chosen for the organization was the Noble and Holy Order of the Knights of Labor. The name was never to be spoken or written. Instead the Knights were referred to in writing by five asterisks (*****). The group tried to bind workers together in a "brotherhood" to gradually improve their lives.

The leader of the new Knights of Labor was Uriah S. Stephens. Born in 1821,

This 1886 lithograph shows early leaders of the Knights of Labor. Terence Powderly is in the center and Samuel Gompers is third from bottom left.

Stephens had studied to be a minister, but because of lack of money he became a garment cutter. Stephens's title in the Knights was "Master Workman." The titles of other officers were Worthy Foreman, Worthy Inspector, and Unknown Knight.

The Knights grew slowly because of the organization's secrecy. A worker might be a member, but a person working in the same shop might never know it. New members were carefully chosen; indeed, they usually didn't know they were being considered for membership.

A person might be invited to a Knights meeting without being told what the meeting was about. Once there, the worker was questioned by the Knights. If the answers about the "elevation of labor" were satisfactory, the person would be asked to join the union.

In August 1870, the Knights decided to allow its members to tell others about the existence of the group. They weren't permitted to reveal who members were, however, or how meetings were run. Soon, the first nontailor was admitted to the Knights.

The seal of the Knights of Labor.

When many members of the same trade joined the Knights, they were allowed to "swarm"—to form an assembly of their own. A second assembly, made up of ship carpenters, was formed in 1872. Over the next two years, eighty more assemblies sprang up in and around Philadelphia, and in 1874 one was formed in New York. Each group was made up of members of distinct crafts—masons, blacksmiths, and so on.

District assemblies, made up of delegates from local assemblies, were the next step in the building of the Knights. The first district assembly was formed in Philadelphia. Assemblies in Camden, New Jersey, and Pittsburgh followed. By 1878, there were district assemblies in the states of Ohio, Indiana, Illinois, West Virginia, New York, New Jersey, and Pennsylvania.

The Knights had about nine thousand members by this time. What is important is that they were workers in *different*

trades. In areas where there weren't enough members of one trade to make an assembly, a "mixed assembly" of skilled as well as unskilled workers was formed.

The leaders thought that the time was right for a national organization. In January 1878, thirty-three delegates from the district assemblies met in Reading, Pennsylvania. The delegates agreed to set up a general assembly to oversee district and local assemblies.

The general assembly never really had supreme authority. Local assemblies often went their own way. Still, the Knights of Labor was now a national organization. It was the first union of working people from many different trades, and it was an organization of individuals, not unions. A worker could now join the Knights simply by applying for membership and paying dues.

Unlike many labor organizations of the day, the Knights of Labor welcomed *all* workers. Membership in the Knights didn't depend on a worker's sex, skin color, or original nationality. In fact, African Americans made up 10 percent of the Knights membership at one time.

The Knights supported boycotts—putting pressure on companies it believed were unfair to employees by not buying their products. To settle labor disputes, the Knights favored arbitration—agreeing to have a "third party" (someone who was neither a worker nor a boss) listen to both sides. The Knights tried to avoid strikes. Such actions had to approved national organization's executive board.

Their aims were ambitious. They demanded an eight-hour workday, equal

The Knights was one of the few early labor organizations to allow African-American workers to join. Here, Grand Master Workman Terence Powderly introduces Frank Farrell, an African-American delegate, to the 1886 Knights convention.

pay for both sexes, and an end to child labor.

By 1879, the Knights had over 28,000 members. In that year, Uriah Stephens resigned as leader of the Knights. Terence V. Powderly was chosen as the new Grand Master Workman.

Powderly, born in Pennsylvania in 1849, didn't look like a leader of working people. He was short, had wavy hair and a droopy mustache, and wore glasses. He looked more like a poet or a college professor than "the leader of million sons of toil."

One of Powderly's first goals was to do away with what was left of the Knights' early secrecy. He believed such secrecy was keeping many workers from joining the organization. In fact, the Roman Catholic Church, which opposed secret societies of any kind, refused to allow its members to join the Knights.

In 1881, the general assembly voted to drop the "Holy and Noble" from the Knights' title and to give up the remaining elements of secrecy. From then on, membership began to climb, reaching more than 100,000 by 1885.

As the Knights' leader, Powderly worked hard—and often complained about how hard he worked. He was, in fact, not a physically strong man. Also, he had many interests outside the Knights of Labor. He was mayor of Scranton, Pennsylvania, when he was elected Grand Master, and he continued in that job until 1884. Powderly was also part owner of a grocery store and vice president of a group called the Irish Land League.

Powderly truly believed in the ideals of the Knights of Labor and continually promoted them. At one point, the national organization bought a coal mine and operated it as a cooperative—a business owned and run by its employees. The workers owned and ran the mine, but unfortunately it wasn't successful. The Knights' mine couldn't compete with commercial mines, and the Knights who ran the mine weren't efficient managers. Much of the Knights' treasury was spent on ventures like this, but none were very successful.

More important to the average member were the issues of working hours and wages. The Knights had to deal with those issues, and when they dealt with them the question of strikes arose. Powderly opposed strikes. In fact, he once boasted: "Not once did I, during my fourteen years [as Grand Master] . . . order a strike."

Strikes, however, were to be the downfall of Terence Powderly and the Knights of Labor.

In 1885, the Wabash Railroad, one of many railroads owned by the powerful businessman Jay Gould, decided it would no longer hire members of the Knights of Labor. In fact, the Wabash started to fire employees who were Knights. Members employed on other railroads owned by Gould asked the Knights' national leaders for permission to strike in sympathy.

Powderly was ill at the time, and leadership was in the hands of the executive board. The national leaders didn't want a strike, but they realized the very life of the organization was being challenged. The executive board allowed the Wabash workers to strike and told members on other railroads not to handle any cars owned by the Wabash system. These actions tied up rail traffic throughout the southwestern states.

Gould finally met with the leaders of the Knights of Labor—Powderly had recovered from his illness—to attempt to end the dispute. It was the first meeting of a powerful businessman with the national leaders of a labor union. In the end, Gould agreed to rehire the fired members of the Knights. Powderly promised not to allow any further strikes against Gould's railroads unless he warned Gould first.

The successful conclusion of the strike led to a huge boost in The Knights' membership. By July 1886, the Knights numbered 729,677, compared with just 100,000 in July 1885.

In February 1886, a member was fired

This cartoon shows financier Jay Gould using Wall Street as a bowling alley.

from the Texas Pacific Railroad, which was owned by Jay Gould. The local assembly of Knights called a strike. This group wasn't as well organized as the Wabash group, and it didn't have as many members. The railroad easily found men to replace the striking workers. By the end of March, the strikers looked to the national organization for help.

Powderly was in a bad bargaining position with Gould. He had promised to warn Gould of any strikes, but this one had been called without his permission. Because of this, Gould didn't think much of Powderly's leadership and refused to give in.

The strike turned violent. Workers and their families went hungry. Frustration over the union's failure to negotiate an agreement led to the strike being called off in May. Workers were becoming unhappy with the Knights of Labor.

Attention Workingmen!

GREAT

MASS-MEETING

TO-NIGHT, at 7.30 o'clock,

AT THE

HAYMARKET, Randolph St, Bet. Desplaines and Halsted.

Good Speakers will be present to denounce the latest atrocious act of the police. the shooting of our fellow-workmen yesterday afternoon.

Workingmen Arm Yourselves and Appear in Full Force!

THE EXECUTIVE COMMITTEE

Achtung, Arbeiter!

Große

Massen-Versammlung

Heute Abend, ½8 Uhr, auf dem

Heumarkt, Randolph-Straße, zwischen Desplaines- u. Halsted-Str.

☞ Gute Redner werden den neuesten Schurkenstreich der Polizei, indem sie gestern Nachmittag unsere Brüder erschoß, geißeln.

☞ Arbeiter, bewaffnet Euch und erscheint massenhaft!

Das Executiv-Comite.

3

DISASTER IN HAYMARKET SQUARE

Most of the labor organizations founded after the Civil War were *trade* unions. They were not particularly strong, but their strength lay in the fact that their members worked in the same trade and had similar interests. Also, because they were skilled workers, they were harder for employers to replace. In 1881, several unions banded together to form the Federation of Organized Trades and Labor Unions of the United States and Canada.

The federation worked mainly to promote laws in Congress favorable to its members. The federation did not last very long, but it was important.

At its annual meeting in 1885, the federation called for a nationwide strike to achieve the eight-hour workday. The idea

Reflecting Chicago's large immigrant population, this poster announcing the meeting in Haymarket Square was printed in English and German.

of a strike stretching across the country for one goal was appealing to workers. The Knights of Labor favored the shortened workday but opposed strikes. It urged its members not to take part—with little success. Local assemblies joined anyway.

May 1, 1886, was set for the beginning of the strike. Workers in New York, Chicago, Milwaukee, and Cincinnati supported the action. Chicago had become the leading city when 62,000 workers announced their support for the strike in April.

May 1 arrived, and there were meetings held all over the country supporting an eight-hour workday. Almost 200,000 people struck the first day. The number grew to 340,000 in the following days.

The McCormick Harvester Company in Chicago had hired workers to replace those out on strike. These people were called scabs by the strikers. Arguments and fights between the striking workers

A newspaper artist's view of the violence in Haymarket Square on May 4, 1886.

and scabs broke out on May 3 at the McCormick factory. The police were called to restore order. As they arrived, gunshots rang out, and a worker fell dead. Several others were wounded.

Radicals, who believed that only violence could achieve the aims of working people, seized on the event to call for a protest meeting to be held the next night. The place for the meeting was Haymarket Square in Chicago. August Spies, the editor of a radical newspaper, was the main speaker.

The mayor of Chicago actually attended the rally for a while, probably to be sure it was peaceful. On the nearby streets were more than 180 policeman.

Speaker followed speaker. One said: "War has been declared upon us; and I ask you to get hold of everything that will help to resist the onslaught of the enemy. What matters it whether you kill yourselves with work to get a little relief, or die on the battle field resisting the enemy?"

Just as the meeting was ending, a detachment of police approached. As the police captain ordered the workers to go home, a bomb was thrown at the group of police. One man died immediately. The police panicked and opened fire on the crowd.

The crowd fled, but not before four workers were killed and about fifty injured. Seven policemen were killed or fatally wounded, and sixty-seven people were injured.

Chicago and the entire country were horrified by the events at Haymarket Square. Newspapers called for the arrest and hanging of the crowd's leaders. Everyone knew radicals were involved, and within days eight people (including Spies) were arrested for the murder of a policeman. Seven were quickly found guilty and condemned to death; the eighth was sentenced to fifteen years in prison.

There was little proof that the convicted men had thrown the bomb at Haymarket Square. (In fact, the identity of the bomb thrower is still unknown.) The eight were arrested and punished because they believed in violence. Ordinary people were scared. The state's attorney pled with the jury: "Convict these men, make examples of them, hang them, and you save our institutions." The fact that most of the accused men were German immigrants played a role, too; many people were prejudiced against immigrants, who were thought to have "radical" ideas.

Four of the condemned men were hanged; one committed suicide in prison. Six years later, the remaining two were pardoned by Illinois Governor John Altgeld. But resentment and distrust of the labor movement lingered on.

Labor unions, including the Knights of Labor, pointed out that they had nothing to do with the violence in Haymarket Square, but people now linked unions with violence anyway. The struggle for the eight-hour day ended. Great damage to labor resulted from the Haymarket meeting.

Of course, some people distrusted labor unions long before the Haymarket Riot, especially the people (almost all of them men) who owned and ran the nation's industries.

The people who owned and operated the nation's major industries were products of their times. Success to most meant gaining wealth, and often it seemed that the way the wealth was gained didn't matter. In this kind of thinking, common in the United States and Europe in the nineteenth century, success was considered its own reward. A person who worked for a living and didn't become rich was useless and did not deserve success. Thus, many successful business people felt that labor unions were interfering with the natural order of things by demanding fewer hours and higher wages.

August Spies and the other radicals responsible for calling the Haymarket meeting were known as anarchists—they believed governments and businesses made slaves of workers, and they wanted to create a society where individuals would enjoy freedom without government. Their beliefs were an outgrowth of the writing of Pierre Proudhon, a Frenchman, who wanted people to share ownership of all property.

Proudhon was not the only European to influence people in the United States. In 1880, almost half a million Europeans came to the United States. By 1890, 5 million more had emigrated from Europe. Many new ideas and theories arrived in the United States with this great wave of people.

Almost all the new theories were forms of *socialism*. Socialism teaches that society should be based on government ownership of the means of production and distribution of goods. In other words, no one person or group should

Within the cartoon:
When two hours is a day's work, with three holidays every week, he will have to take plenty of exercise, to keep in good physical condition.

He will travel, in order to compare his own condition with that of the European workingman.

Doubtless he will employ some of his leisure in writing essays on the condition of things in general.

He will elect himself to Congress, and look after his condition there, personally.

And, of course, by that time, everything will be in such a condition that Fashionable Society will welcome him with open arms.

F. Opper

This cartoon, "The American Workingman of the Future," pokes fun at organized labor's attempts to improve the quality of life of American workers.

own a company or control an industry. Everyone should have a part in it.

There were spokespeople for these various points of view. A German named Karl Marx (who wrote a column for the *New York Tribune* in the 1860s) believed, "History of all society is the history of class struggle." Marx believed workers in all countries should unite to run all businesses and industries.

The Frenchman Charles Fourier believed in forming small socialist communities where workers worked toward a common benefit. He hoped to recreate a simpler society—like the one before the Industrial Revolution.

Ferdinand Lasalle was another socialist who was a hero to many immigrant workers. He believed government should encourage a socialist society by taking over and running important industries.

All these people contributed to the ideas of some members of the labor movement in the United States. They all recognized the kinship of workers and their common problems. But their ideas did not direct the American labor movement. The United States was not a fertile ground for socialism. American workers were to find their own way. In the years ahead, Samuel Gompers would help show them how.

4

THE BIRTH OF THE AFL

Making cigars was one way of earning money in New York City in the 1870s. Many people were engaged in this trade: men, women, and children. Some worked in shops, but many more worked in dark, cramped apartments called tenements. There were only 131 members in local cigarmakers' unions.

When he was ten years old, Samuel Gompers learned to make cigars from his father. At first he worked at home, a tenement apartment located between a slaughterhouse and a brewery on New York's Lower East Side. He and his father soon got jobs working in shops.

Young Gompers went to work for David Hirsch, who ran a union shop, in 1873. It was here that he received his union education. Cigarmaking shops were large rooms filled with hard benches and long, low tables. The workers sat on the benches and rolled to-

Federal troops escort mail trains out of the Chicago railroad yards during the Pullman Strike of 1894.

bacco leaves into cigars on the tables. Making cigars was a skill that was not mastered easily, but once it was, it became boring.

To make the work interesting, the workers in David Hirsch's shop chose one of their number to read aloud from labor magazines or newspapers. Sam Gompers was often selected to be the reader. Because a worker was paid by the number of cigars he made each day, the workers in the shop would chip in a certain number of cigars to make up the reader's pay.

Items from a newspaper or magazine usually led the workers into long discussions about labor reforms or politics. These discussions were fascinating for young Samuel Gompers. He read as much as he could about labor unions and began to form opinions of his own. Gompers believed that a union should be concerned with improving the welfare of its workers and not with reforming society as a whole. In other words, it should stick to improving the lot of the workers

Samuel Gompers's membership card in the Cigar Maker's International Union.

and not get involved in politics or any other side issue.

Gompers became interested in making the cigarmakers' union stronger. Together with Adolph Strasser and Ferdinand Laurrell, he worked to increase membership in the union and strengthen its policies. In November 1875, a New York local was chartered by the Cigarmakers International Union, with Gompers as its president. Two years later, Strasser was elected president of the international organization.

One concern of the new union was the workers in the tenements who went on strike in 1877. These workers were at the mercy of their employers, who were often also their landlords. They worked from early morning to late at night, scarcely stopping to eat. In bad times, they lost their jobs and often their homes as well. And 1877 was a bad time: the nation was still in the grip of an economic depression that had begun in 1873.

The Cigarmakers International Union tried to help these striking workers by setting up soup kitchens to feed them and by finding them new places to live. They even set up a cooperative shop to employ those out of work. Gompers quit his job to run this shop.

To force the cigarmakers to give up, employers closed their doors for a time. With all the cigarmakers now out of work, support for the strike weakened.

As the strike slowly fell apart, employers reopened their shops and workers went back. Sam Gompers, however, couldn't find a job for a long time. No one would hire him because of his activities during the strike. In other words, he was blacklisted.

The Cigarmakers International Union was determined to survive and succeed. Only the international organization could authorize a strike. It charged dues and other fees that were set aside to help during strikes. If one local was on strike, other locals could be ordered to help with their own strike funds. It kept both authority and discipline centralized. No strike would be authorized unless the union was sure it would be successful.

Many of the Cigarmakers were also members of the Knights of Labor, including Gompers. The Knights of Labor was a diverse organization. It had assemblies of trades, national unions, industries, and regional groups. Skilled workers—like those in the Cigarmakers Union—were uncomfortable with some of the unskilled workers' unions that made up the Knights' membership.

This dissatisfaction with the Knights wasn't new. As early as 1881, in Pittsburgh, 107 trade union delegates had gathered to form a new organization, called the Federation of Organized Trades and Labor Unions of the United States and Canada. They wanted independence from the Knights' control. But the Knights' leadership wasn't willing to grant them that independence. The new organization never gained wide support or attracted many members.

In New York City, arguments in the Cigarmaker's union led one group to leave the organization. The group joined the Knights of Labor, angering the remaining members of the Cigarmakers International Union.

In May 1886, leaders of trade unions met in Philadelphia to work out a stronger organization. They believed that the Knights of Labor was out to destroy trade unions as such. The trade-union leaders put together a list of demands for the Knights to consider. One demand called for the Knights to drop their trade

Adolph Strasser, Gompers's friend and fellow union official.

assemblies. Another was that a member of a trade union not be allowed to join the Knights of Labor without the trade union's permission.

The Knights refused even to negotiate any of these demands. In fact, the Knights continued to authorize trade assemblies.

The trade unions then called for a convention to organize a "trades congress." The convention met in Columbus, Ohio, in December 1886. The purpose of the meeting was to pull "the bonds of unity much closer together between all the trades unions."

Unhappy with the attitude of the Knights of Labor, 42 delegates, who represented 317,000 trade union members, decided to establish a new organization

Workers hold a rally in New York City to support striking railroad workers.

exclusively for trade unions. The organization was to be called the American Federation of Labor (AFL).

The Federation of Organized Trades and Labor Unions was meeting in Pittsburgh at the same time. The federation decided to disband and give all its money—less than $300—to the AFL. The federation's leaders also asked its membership to join the newly created AFL.

The AFL convention drew up a constitution setting the organization's goals: encouraging the formation of unions, aiding member unions, and securing laws favorable to working people. The AFL constitution also set strict guidelines. Only one union would represent each trade, and a worker who wanted to join an AFL union had to be "favorable to trades unions."

The convention set up an executive council to lead the AFL. Only one of its members—Samuel Gompers, the president—would work full-time for the or-

ganization. Gompers was to be responsible for the AFL's day-to-day operations.

Gompers immediately set up a national headquarters for the AFL in New York City. The organization gave him $160.52 for this purpose. The Cigar Makers International donated a tiny room for an office, and Gompers supplied his family's kitchen table for a desk. Boxes were used as chairs, and crates for file cabinets.

From this headquarters Gompers wrote constantly to labor leaders around the country persuading them to join the AFL. He also published a newspaper for a time, issued charters, collected dues, and went on organizing and speaking tours. By the time of its second convention, membership in the AFL had almost doubled, to 600,000.

At the heart of the AFL was its philosophy not to interfere in the internal affairs of its member unions. Each trade was independent. The central office issued

The founding committee of the American Federation of Labor. Samuel Gompers is standing at left.

This lithograph shows New York City about the time Gompers opened the AFL's main office there.

charters to member unions and settled disputes between unions. Each union paid a "tax" to support a central fund to be used during strikes. The AFL helped national or international unions win recognition from employers and bargain for better wages, hours, and working conditions. It supported a union in the case of a strike. A union could exist without the AFL, but the AFL could not exist without its member unions.

The founding and growth of the American Federation of Labor was encouraging to many workers, but there were still dark days ahead. The 1890s were a time of defeat and sometimes despair for American labor.

In 1892, the members of the Amalgamated Association of Iron, Steel and Tin workers refused to accept wage cuts at the Carnegie Steel Company plant in Homestead, Pennsylvania. Henry Clay Frick, chairman of the board of Carnegie Steel, fired eight hundred men. He planned to begin a *lockout*—deliberately closing down the plant in order to break the union.

Frick refused to talk to union leaders, and he surrounded the plant with a high fence with barbed wire at the top. Union leaders were sure that this meant he was going to bring in strikebreakers to run the plant. Rumors got around that Frick had called on the Pinkerton Detective Agency for help.

He had. On July 6, 1892, two barges carrying three hundred "Pinkertons" approached Homestead. Gunfire broke out. The striking workers had gathered

A newspaper illustration shows striking steel workers battling Pinkerton guards at Homestead, Pennsylvania.

along the Monongahela River to challenge the Pinkertons and to stop them from going ashore. The Pinkertons returned fire and two strikers were killed.

The Pinkertons withdrew to the barges, which drifted to the middle of the river. All day long, from four in the morning until five at night, the battle continued. At one point, the strikers poured oil on the river and set it on fire. They brought in an old cannon and tried to sink the barges, but they were unsuccessful. Finally, a white flag was raised from a barge. The Pinkertons said they would surrender if they were allowed to go ashore and leave Homestead. The strikers accepted the Pinkertons' offer.

On July 12, the governor of Pennsylvania sent a division of the National Guard to Homestead to restore order. The Carnegie Company, feeling secure with such protection, began to bring in non-union workers. It also started lawsuits against the leaders of the union, charging murder and incitement (encouraging people) to riot.

The Amalgamated Iron, Steel and Tin Workers Union was a member of the AFL, and Samuel Gompers visited Homestead to encourage the strikers. The AFL contributed $7,000 to their cause. But it was all in vain. By November, the workers had lost hope in gaining their objectives, and on November 21 about five hundred strikers applied for work at the Homestead plant.

Twenty-two hundred workers had gone on strike; only 406 were rehired. Workers lost almost $850,000 in wages during the strike, and the state of Pennsylvania spent over $400,000. It was a major setback for American labor. But an even bigger disaster for labor lay ahead—the Pullman Strike.

Workers at the Pullman Palace Car Company were said to be lucky. After all, they lived in a model town—Pullman,

The Pinkertons

God help them tonight in the hour of their affliction,
Praying for him who they'll ne'er meet again
Hear the poor orphans tell their sad story,
Father was killed by the Pinkerton men.

How did the Pinkertons, a well-known and highly respected detective agency, get involved with the Homestead mess? Why did Frick call in detectives?

The answer is: He didn't.

Allen Pinkerton, a Scottish immigrant, set up Pinkerton's National Detective Agency in 1850 after a series a successful detecting jobs. The agency grew quickly in a country that had no large police forces. It earned respect by sticking doggedly to a job until it was done. The Pinkerton National Detective Agency lived up to its motto, "We Never Sleep."

During the Civil War, Pinkerton investigated threats of sabotage to railroads by Confederate sympathizers. He even uncovered and foiled a plot to assassinate President-elect Abraham Lincoln. Pinkerton tried his hand as a Union spy, without much success.

After Pinkerton's death, his two sons carried on the business. It was they who came up with the idea of providing guard service as well as detective service. Guards were not on the regular payroll of the agency. When someone contracted for guards, the agency hired people indiscriminately. These new people had no special training. The 396 men on the barges on the Monongahela River were hired by the Pinkertons after Frick asked the agency to guard the Homestead steel plant. The men were hired just for that job. The "Pinkertons" on the barges were guards, not detectives.

Illinois, just twelve miles from Chicago. Pullman was a company town. George Pullman, founder of the company, had bought four thousand acres of land and had built a town, complete with houses, stores, church, theater, library, and school. His idea was to keep his company (which made railroad passenger cars) and its employees in one place.

But Pullman, Illinois, was not a "worker's paradise." Rent was deducted from a worker's paycheck; food had to be bought at the company store. Books could be checked out of the library, but there was a membership fee that many could not afford. Rents for apartments were 25 percent higher than in neighboring towns. A rival businessman did not think much of the model town. He suggested Pullman sold water and gas at a huge profit. A Pullman employee once said, "We are born in a Pullman house, fed from the Pullman shop, taught in the Pullman school . . . and when we die we shall be buried in the Pullman cemetery and go to the Pullman hell."

The year 1893 was not a good one for the Pullman Company. Because of another severe economic depression, orders fell off for luxury railroad cars. Prices for the cars were lowered in the hope that business would pick up. George Pullman asked his workers to accept lower wages, and they did. Some workers made 40 percent less than before, but there was no reduction in rents and food prices.

In May 1894, a delegation of workers met George Pullman and asked him to raise their wages or lower their rents. Pullman insisted that the company was still losing money and therefore couldn't raise wages. As for the rents, he said he didn't believe the company's real estate had anything to do with the railroad-car company. He considered them separate businesses.

The next day three of the workers who had talked with Pullman were fired. All three were members of the American Railway Union. The Pullman locals called a strike to protest the firings. The company answered the strike with a lockout.

The American Railway Union answered the appeal of the Pullman locals and supported the strike. If the Pullman Company did not negotiate, union leaders warned, its members would refuse to work on trains containing Pullman cars.

The company refused to negotiate. Union workers cut Pullman cars from trains and sidetracked them. Many railroads stopped running because they had no sleeping cars. In three days, 125,000 workers on twenty railroads struck in support of the Pullman workers.

The managers of the railroads ordered the firing of any worker who cut a Pullman car from a train. The order backfired. Every time a man was fired, the entire train crew would quit.

Railroad traffic into and out of Chicago ground to a halt. So did another kind of traffic: the United States mail, which relied on railroad transportation in those days before trucks and airplanes. The postmaster general in Washington received reports from around the country of mail shipments stopped because of the strike.

Strikebreakers—men hired by the

Illinois National Guard troops fire at strikers in the Chicago rail yards on July 7, 1894.

railroads to take the strikers' places—were sworn in as special deputies by the Illinois attorney general. Clashes between these "deputies" and strikers resulted, and rioting broke out. On July 2, 1894, the federal marshal in Chicago telegraphed the attorney general in Washington. He warned that local forces couldn't stop the rioting, and he asked for help.

President Grover Cleveland sent four companies of federal troops to Chicago. Violence continued when trains began to move under the soldiers' protection. People around the country were shocked by newspaper reports of riots and looting. The *New York Tribune* called the strike "the greatest battle between labor and capital that has ever been inaugurated in the United States."

Judge Peter Grosscup of the federal district court issued a blanket injunction (court order) forbidding anyone to interfere with the mails.

Facing these powerful forces, the American Railway Union faltered. It appealed to the American Federation of Labor to call a general strike: a strike where all union members would withhold their labor from any company, whether it was a railroad or not. The AFL, under Gompers's leadership, refused. They felt that a general strike was too powerful a weapon to use carelessly.

The Pullman strike collapsed.

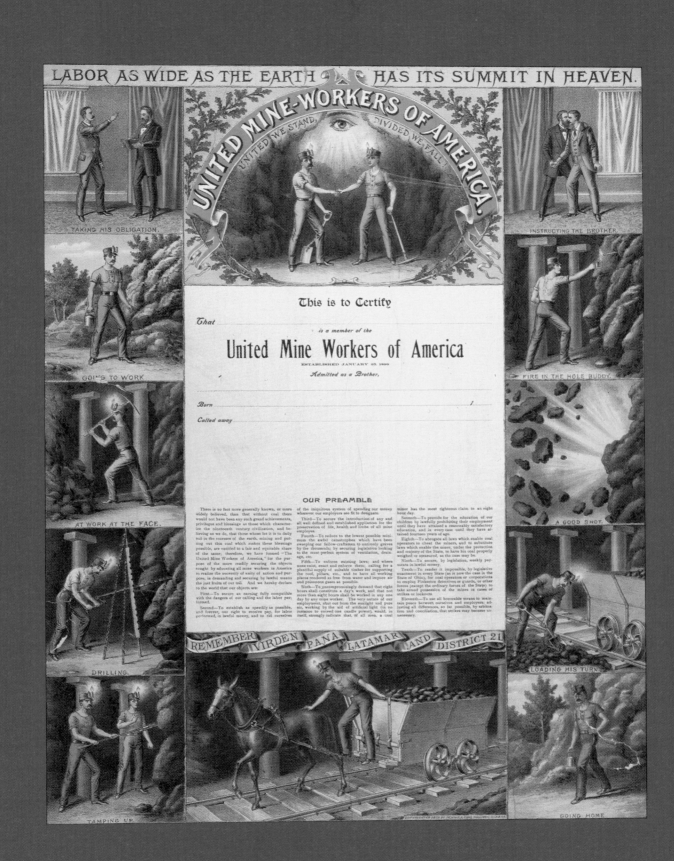

5

DECADES OF GROWTH AND CONFLICT

The American Federation of Labor grew during the 1880s and 1890s, but only among workers in specific trades. The AFL was a collection of trade unions. Unskilled workers were not welcome as members.

Unskilled workers had to face another problem: the huge flow of immigrants from overseas. The newcomers to the United States were eager to work and were not particular about wages or working conditions. Unskilled workers were at a disadvantage when it came to unionizing: If they tried to strike or form a union, they could easily be replaced.

The AFL was not too concerned about the plight of unskilled workers, and it moved slowly to support limiting the flow of immigrants. After all, Samuel Gompers and other leaders of the AFL were immigrants or the children of immigrants.

An 1899 membership certificate of the United Mine Workers Union.

But then immigrants from China and other nations began arriving in the United States with marketable skills. These skilled immigrants, many trade-union leaders believed, threatened jobs for union members. In 1906, the AFL called on Congress to keep Chinese immigrants out of the country and restrict the numbers of immigrants from other countries.

On paper at least, the AFL didn't discriminate against workers of any race, but many of the organization's leaders didn't enforce equality within member unions. Gompers tried to persuade unions to accept African American members at first. But it was a time when discrimination against African Americans was widespread. Gompers wanted to win public acceptance for the AFL, and so he tried to avoid controversial issues, including racial equality. In his 1890 report to the AFL, Gompers insisted that the union recognize the "necessity of avoiding as far as possible all controversial questions." Sometime in the 1890s, Gompers gave up

This picture, titled "In the Factory," shows a typical workplace of the early 1900s—smoky, grimy, and potentially dangerous.

and turned a blind eye toward this kind of discrimination.

One of the largest member unions of the AFL was the United Mine Workers Union, headed by John Mitchell. The Mine Workers were strong in the bituminous coal fields of Pennsylvania, Ohio, Indiana, and Michigan, but it was not successful in organizing the anthracite coal miners in eastern Pennsylvania. (There are two kinds of coal: bituminous is soft, while anthracite is hard and burns more cleanly than bituminous.)

The anthracite fields were mostly owned by railroads that used the coal to fuel their trains. The railroads were usually hostile toward unions. The miners in the coalfields worked ten hours a day, underground. Deadly accidents were common, and most miners earned less than $300 a year.

John Mitchell and the United Mine Workers (UMW) tried to make conditions better and raise wages. In 1902, the UMW called a strike, and mine owners responded with a vengeance. They called in thousands of their own police, hired special deputies, and began hiring scabs. They also charged the union with rioting and sabotage.

There was little basis for these charges. Most of the miners stayed off the job and didn't engage in violence. John Mitchell—a miner from the age of twelve—was a wise and patient leader. He was willing to compromise with the owners on a settlement, but the owners refused to talk at all.

The strike dragged on, and shortages of coal began to appear around the country. At first, the public sympathized with the owners. But as time went on, and the owners refused to talk at all with the union, they began to support the workers. President Theodore Roosevelt personally traveled to eastern Pennsylvania to visit the strikers.

President Roosevelt was concerned about the coal shortage and called a conference of mine owners and union leaders at the White House. At this meeting, Mitchell agreed to abide by any reasonable compromise. However, the owners refused to talk. Their attitude annoyed the president.

Roosevelt drew up a plan to have the U.S. Army take over the operation of the mines. The secretary of war told the owners about Roosevelt's plan and said it would take effect if they didn't agree to arbitration.

The owners reluctantly agreed to abide by the decision of an arbitrating committee. They insisted, however, that they approve the members of the committee. They also demanded that no union member be on the committee. They wanted the committee members to include, among others, a judge, a businessman, and a sociologist.

The AFL and other unions fought to put an end to child labor. Many children (like the textile worker above) worked long hours in unsafe workplaces well into the twentieth century.

John Mitchell (left), president of the American Mine Workers Union, with Samuel Gompers.

Roosevelt was stumped for a while, but he came up with a way to represent labor's side on the committee. He appointed E. E. Clark as the sociologist, "a man who has thought and studied deeply on social questions and has practically applied his knowledge." The way Clark applied his knowledge just happened to be as head of the Order of Railway Conductors—a union. Eventually the committee ended the strike by awarding the workers a 10 percent raise and reducing their working hours. But the settlement did not order the mine owners to recognize the union, and the mine owners simply raised the price of coal to make up for the miners' raise.

This marked the first time a president had intervened in a labor dispute on the side of labor in the United States.

In another area of labor, the United Hatters Union tried to organize the workers of D. E. Loewe & Company in Danbury, Connecticut. When its strike failed, the United Hatters started a boycott of Loewe's hats. The boycott was so successful that it cost the company about $100,000. The company sued the United Hatters Union, saying the union broke the law by "conspiring to restrain trade."

After years of arguing, the courts found in favor of D. E. Loewe & Company and fined the United Hatters $252,000. Only with help from the AFL was the union able to pay off the fine.

More trouble over boycotts arose when Gompers listed Buck's Stove and Range Company on the AFL's "We Don't Patronize" list. This list of companies considered unfair to organized labor was published in the AFL's magazine *American Federationist*. Buck's Stove was listed because the company's president had refused to negotiate with union members.

Buck's Stove immediately went to court and got an order forbidding Gompers and the AFL to continue listing it. They refused to obey the court's order. Then Gompers and his colleagues were charged with contempt of court for not obeying the order. Gompers was even sentenced to a prison term, but appealed the case successfully and didn't have to go to jail.

Woodrow Wilson, who turned out to be a friend of labor, was elected president of the United States in 1912. He appointed the first secretary of labor, William B. Wilson. In 1914, President Wilson signed the Clayton Anti-Trust Act into law.

The Clayton Act supported the dignity of the worker and stated that labor unions were not "illegal combinations." It also recognized the legality of strikes, picketing, and boycotts. Samuel Gompers hailed the act as a major step forward for organized labor.

The United States entered World War I in 1917. Gompers was an enthusiastic supporter of the war effort. He was a member of the Council of National Defense, a group organized to see that labor and management disputes didn't affect defense industries. As a reward, President Wilson named Gompers chairman of the Commission on International Labor Legislation when the war was over.

This was Samuel Gompers's last triumph. After the end of World War I, his hold over the American Federation of Labor gradually weakened. For years,

DEVOTED TO THE INTERESTS AND VOICING THE DEMANDS OF THE TRADE UNION MOVEMENT

Vol. XIII.   MAY, 1906.   No.

LABOR'S BILL OF GRIEVANCES

HEADQUARTERS AMERICAN FEDERATION OF LABOR.

WASHINGTON, D. C. *April 7, 1906.*

To All Trade Unionists of America.

DEAR SIRS AND BROTHERS: The Bill of Grievances, printed below, formulated and adopted by the Executive Council of the American Federation of Labor, is expressive of the decision which organized labor of America has made manifest in its various conventions and union meetings. The presidents of all affiliated international unions were invited to meet the Executive Council at the headquarters of the American Federation of Labor, March 21, 1906, and participate in a conference concerning matters affecting labor's interests congressionally and administratively. The presidents or their duly credentialed representatives participated, and unanimously and enthusiastically endorsed and signed the document and participated with the Executive Council in the presentation and reading thereof.

Some garbled accounts of this matter have appeared in the press. In order that our fellow trade unionists may be in possession of the document in its original form, and that their actions may conform thereto, this is presented to you in its entirety.

Let the inspiring watchword go forth that—

We will stand by our friends and administer a stinging rebuke to men or parties who
(293)

A 1906 issue of the American Federationist, *the AFL's newspaper.*

Gompers was almost automatically elected president of the AFL. But in 1921, the president of the United Mine Workers, John L. Lewis, ran against Gompers and received a third of the votes.

Samuel Gompers died in 1924. He had been a union man for almost sixty-five years and had contributed mightily to the union cause in the United States. His guiding philosophy was very simple: "More."

Even before Gompers's death, however, several other labor organizations had struggled for recognition. The

Samuel Gompers (center) with President Woodrow Wilson (left) and William Wilson (right), the first secretary of labor, in 1913.

American Federation of Labor was far from the only union in the United States. There were many labor organizations around the country that were not members of the federation.

The American Railway Union, so active in the Pullman strike, was one such group. Its leader was Eugene V. Debs, a firm believer in industrial unions. He had been a member of the Brotherhood of Locomotive Firemen (workers who kept steam locomotives fueled) for years and had become convinced that firemen alone could not achieve their goals for a better life. The way to achieve these goals was to unite with other railroad workers: engineers, conductors, yard workers, and others. Thus was born the American Railway Union.

Debs went to jail for his part in the Pullman strike. He spent his time there reading and thinking. When he emerged, he was a different man. He now believed that the only way to help the working people of the United States was through radical change. Only by changing the structure of the government, decided Debs, could workers achieve their goals.

Debs went into jail a labor leader; he emerged a politician. In 1897, he helped form the Socialist party and ran for president on its ticket five times. Debs was outspoken in his criticism of trade unions and vigorously supported organizing labor by industry.

Some members of the AFL supported the Socialist party and its goals. Samuel Gompers didn't, and he made sure the

The Past is Behind Us
The Future is Ahead
Let us all strive to
make the future
better and brighter
than the past ever was.

U.S. DEPARTMENT OF LABOR

W.B. WILSON.
Secretary of Labor

A World War I poster promotes unity between labor and government by showing a worker and a soldier clasping hands.

FOR PRESIDENT

EUGENE V. DEBS

A Debs campaign poster from the 1920 election.

AFL stayed out of the party and vice versa. As early as 1894, at the AFL's annual convention, he convinced the AFL leadership to ignore requests for the union's endorsement of socialism. Under Gompers's leadership, the AFL stuck to a program of what was called "pure and simple," or "bread and butter," unionism. Unlike the socialists, the AFL believed that the privately owned industrial economy of the United States was here to stay. It was up to the AFL, Gompers felt, to win better conditions for workers by working within the system, not by trying to change it.

The entry of the United States into World War I in 1917 also highlighted the differences between Gompers's AFL and the socialists. The Socialist party didn't support the war, and neither did Debs. Debs protested not only the war but laws passed by Congress to silence such protest. Debs was arrested, charged with sedition (working to aid the country's enemy), and sentenced to ten years in jail. While still there, in 1920, he again ran for president and received almost a million votes. His supporters wore campaign buttons saying, "For President . . . Convict No. 9653." Just before Christmas, 1921, President Warren Harding ordered Debs released. On the other hand, Gompers supported the war effort, including serving on President Wilson's Council of National Defense.

Many people inside and outside the labor movement disagreed with Debs and his socialist views. But in the early part of the twentieth century, some labor groups took an even more radical course than Debs.

After a violent and unsuccessful strike at Cripple Creek, Colorado, the Western Federation of Miners looked for a strong national organization to join. It became a member of the American Federation of Labor, but withdrew after a short time.

The miners decided to set up another national organization of industrial unions. A meeting was called in Chicago in 1905.

Eugene Debs from the Socialist party came. Daniel De Leon, a college professor who had started the Socialist Trade and Labor Alliance, represented his group. In all, there were labor leaders representing about 140,000 workers.

The meeting was called to order by William Dudley ("Big Bill") Haywood of the Western Federation of Miners. He set the tone of the group when he said, "This is the Continental Congress of the working class. We are here to confederate the workers of this country into a movement that shall have for its purpose the emancipation of the working class from the slave bondage of capitalism."

The Industrial Workers of the World, more commonly known as the Wobblies, was born.

Haywood was a product of the wild West. He had worked at various times as a miner, rancher, and farmer. He was an eager convert to unionism and rose to power in the Western Federation of Miners. Haywood was used to a rough and tumble life, and he didn't mind using violent tactics in a strike if it seemed they were needed.

Before devoting full time and attention on the new organization, however, Haywood had to face another problem. Along with two other men, Haywood was accused of conspiring to kill former Idaho governor Frank Steunenberg. He spent over a year in jail waiting for his trial.

The *Haywood* case became a rallying point for workers all over the country. Many believed that Haywood was accused of murder only because of his union activities. Steunenberg had dealt harshly with strikes during his time as governor. Clarence Darrow, the most famous lawyer of his time, defended Haywood.

"Big Bill" Haywood, leader of the Industrial Workers of the World.

In 1907, Haywood was found not guilty.

In the meantime, the IWW was struggling with internal problems. Because of its diverse membership, there were arguments over policy, structure, and politics. These were finally resolved, but not before Debs and De Leon had left. The Western Federation of Miners withdrew, but Haywood stayed on.

After this wrangling, there were only about six thousand members left in the IWW, but they were firmly committed to the union cause. They set out to make converts among anyone who would

The Singing Union

The Wobblies were a colorful group. They were mostly young (except for Mary Harris, better known as Mother Jones, who was seventy-five years old at the time of the founding convention) and eager to fight for "One Big Union."

One of these young people, Joe Hill (born Joe Hillström in Sweden) captured the spirit and caught the imagination of the group. He also made a lasting contribution to American culture. Joe Hill wrote songs. Tune into a folk music program on the radio today and you might hear one of his songs. Among them are "Solidarity Forever" sung to the tune of the Civil War song "John Brown's Body":

> It is we who plowed the prairies, built the cities where they trade,
> Dug the mines and built the workshops; endless miles of railroad laid,
> Now we stand outcast and starving, 'mid the wonders we have made
> But the union makes us strong.
> Solidarity forever! Solidarity forever! Solidarity forever!
> The union makes us strong!

A favorite of the Wobblies was "The Preacher and the Slave," a song that parodies a Salvation Army hymn "In the Sweet Bye and Bye":

> Long-haired preachers come out every night,
> Try to tell you what's wrong and what's right;
> But when asked how 'bout something to eat
> They will answer with voices so sweet:
> You will eat, bye and bye,
> In that glorious land above the sky;
> Work and pray, live on hay,
> You'll get pie in the sky when you die.

Joe Hill was convicted of murder and executed in 1915. His last telegram to IWW headquarters said, "Don't waste time mourning—organize!"

Hill's songs were collected in the IWW's *Little Red Song Book* and were sung everywhere and anywhere Wobblies gathered. Samuel Gompers, no friend of the radical Wobblies, once sneered that it was a "singing union."

listen. They wandered the country touting the praises of "One Big Union."

Wobblies tried to organize lumberjacks in the Pacific Northwest, farm workers in the South, and immigrant factory workers in the East. People became to be fearful and suspicious of the Wobblies and their tactics.

It was in Lawrence, Massachusetts, in 1912 that the Wobblies had their most notable victory. Workers in the city's textile mills walked off the job when they received a pay cut. About 30,000 workers went on strike in Lowell, only some 300 of them IWW members. The small IWW local found itself the organizing group behind the strike—a job its leaders didn't feel they could handle.

Help arrived in the form of Big Bill Haywood. Although it was out of character for him, he advised a calm approach. He felt that nonviolence was the best tactic in this situation. And it was.

It was the mill owners and the police who turned to violence against the strikers. Attacks on strikers and their families led to a public outcry around the country. The owners gave in, reopened the mills, and announced a pay increase.

When World War I broke out in Europe, the IWW took a firm stand against the war. It declared, "We, as members of the industrial army, will refuse to fight for any purposed except for the realization of industrial freedom." When the United States entered the war, the IWW didn't change its stand.

This led to more hard feeling against it than before. Wobblies were seen as unpatriotic, even treasonous. Many

This drawing protests the decision of the city of Lawrence, Massachusetts, not to allow the children of striking textile workers to be sent to friendly homes outside Lawrence.

states outlawed the IWW. The federal government passed laws that sent 160 people, including several radical labor leaders, to prison. Haywood was convicted of sedition (conspiring against the government) and sentenced to twenty years in prison.

While out on bail in 1921, Haywood decided to leave the country. The Russian Revolution had taken place a few years earlier, and word of the "workers' paradise" that the Communists were supposed to be building appealed to him.

He was to be disappointed, but there was no returning to the United States. Big Bill Haywood died in Moscow in 1928.

AFTERWORD

FROM THE AFL TO THE AFL-CIO

Labor unions in the early twentieth century were still proving themselves. They had powerful enemies in the business community—the U.S. Steel Corporation, for example, which was strongly antiunion. But most people eventually began to approve of labor unions and their role in American society.

In 1929, the stock market crashed. The Great Depression resulted. By 1933, nearly 14 million workers were unemployed. The federal government acted.

Congress passed the Norris-LaGuardia Act in 1932. The law contained some sections favorable to organized labor. For instance, it limited the power of the courts to issue injunctions against peaceful strikes. The act also outlawed "yellow dog" contracts—contracts in which an employee had to promise never to join a

George Meany of the AFL and Walter Reuther of the CIO clasp hands to symbolize the merger of the two organizations on December 12, 1955.

union. The National Industrial Recovery Act went into effect in June 1933. Among its provisions was the adoption of a "code of fair practices" for each industry. Noteworthy for labor was that almost all the codes outlawed child labor, specified a forty-hour work week, and set pay scales at between $12 and $15 a week.

About 95 percent of American industries adopted these codes. Unions were delighted with the section of the National Industrial Recovery Act that guaranteed workers the right to bargain collectively with their employers. (Collective bargaining means that workers can join together to negotiate with employers.)

There were flaws in NIRA, however. In 1935, the Supreme Court ruled the act unconstitutional.

Congress acted swiftly to preserve labor's gains. Under the leadership of Senator Robert Wagner of New York, it passed the National Labor Relations Act. This law, often called the Wagner Act,

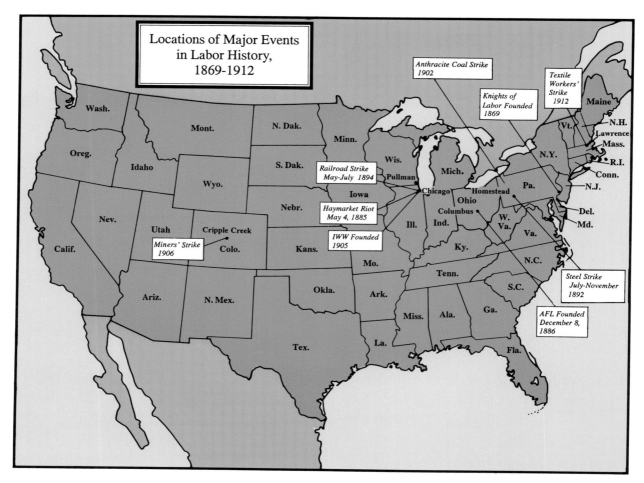

Locations of Major Events
in Labor History,
1869-1912

Anthracite Coal Strike
1902

Knights of
Labor Founded
1869

Textile
Workers'
Strike
1912

Railroad Strike
May-July 1894

Haymarket Riot
May 4, 1885

IWW Founded
1905

Miners' Strike
1906

Steel Strike
July-November
1892

AFL Founded
December 8,
1886

again confirmed the right of workers to bargain collectively. The act also made it illegal for employees to discriminate against union members in hiring.

Membership in unions began to rise with the encouragement of the Wagner Act. John L. Lewis of the United Mine Workers led the move to promote the unionization of "heavy" industries like coal, oil, and steel. In 1935, the Committee for Industrial Organization (CIO) formed to promote this goal. It planned to work within the AFL to encourage industrial unionism. The CIO helped workers in the automobile, steel, and other industries to form unions. These new unions included almost all the workers—skilled and un-skilled—in each industry.

Like trade unionism before it, industrial unionism quickly ran into stiff opposition from many employers, especially automobile manufacturers. In response to this opposition, industrial unions developed a new tactic—the "sit-down" strike. A sit-down strike was the opposite of the usual strike. Instead of staying away from work, the strikers "sat down" on the job and refused to leave until a settlement had been negotiated. The best-known sit-down strikes took place in 1937, when workers at Chrysler and General Motors plants struck until the automakers recognized their union, the new United Automobile Workers Union (UAW).

Steelworkers were not so lucky. In 1937, the Steel Workers Organizing

Committee formed to unionize the steel industry. The nation's biggest steel manufacturer, U.S. Steel, (called Big Steel by the press) agreed to recognize the new union. Smaller companies, called Little Steel, did not. One of the Little Steel companies was Republic Steel. On Memorial Day, 1937, violence broke out between strikers and police at Republic's South Chicago plant. Ten strikers were killed and dozens more wounded. Angry workers called the incident the "Republic Massacre." Finally, the federal government stepped in to help resolve the conflict.

Republic and the other Little Steel companies recognized the union in 1941.

The AFL felt threatened by the growth of the CIO and the new, nontraditional unions. AFL leaders ordered it to disband. When it didn't, they expelled the CIO unions from the AFL.

Undaunted, the CIO reorganized itself as the Congress of Industrial Organizations in 1938 and elected John L. Lewis its president. By 1940, the CIO equaled the membership of the AFL; each had about 3.5 million members.

In response to the growing importance

A cartoon from the 1930s criticizes the attitude of supporters of craft (trade) unions over industrial unions like the CIO.

of organized labor in the 1930s, President Franklin D. Roosevelt proposed the Fair Labor Standards Act in 1937. This law provided for the minimum wage and a maximum work week.

Encouraging as the gains of the 1930s were to organized labor, there was still one group left outside the mainstream: the African-American worker.

A. Philip Randolph, leader of the Brotherhood of Sleeping Car Porters, was becoming more and more frustrated at discrimination against African Americans in employment.

When World War II began, American factories began to work furiously to fill orders from overseas and from the U.S. government. The unemployment rate dropped. But many industries still refused to open up jobs for African Americans. One company, North American Aviation, went so far as to say: "Regardless of their training...we will not employ them."

The federal government didn't seem interested in the discrimination practiced by the companies it was doing business with. In 1941, frustrated with President Roosevelt and Congress for their failure to guarantee equal access to jobs in defense industries, Randolph threatened to lead a march of ten thousand people through the streets of Washington.

In response, Roosevelt set up the Fair Employment Practices Committee (FEPC) to make sure that government contracts were not awarded to businesses that discriminated against African Americans. Critics weren't satisfied with the FEPC, which was headed by a white person and not funded by Congress. In practice, it turned out that FEPC achieved equality only in places where African-American workers and the community put pressure on employers.

The entry of the United States into World War II in 1941 slowed the gains made on the union front. During the war, employers and employees put their differences aside in order to focus on winning the war.

When the war was over, arguments again arose over wages, working conditions, and benefits. Two major strikes took place in 1946: one in the railroad industry and the other in the coal mining industry.

President Harry Truman, while generally a friend of labor, intervened directly to end each of these strikes. He threatened to draft the striking railroad workers into the army, had the federal government seize the coal mines, and obtained an injunction against the striking miners.

These strikes caused a reaction against organized labor and resulted in the passage of the Taft-Hartley Act (Labor-Management Relations Act) in 1947. This law attempted to limit some of the power of the unions. For example, it outlawed closed shop contracts,which permitted only union members to be hired. It also gave the president the power to call for a "cooling-off" period of eighty days before a union called a strike that might affect the nation's safety and security.

The Taft-Hartley Act also gave states the power to outlaw union shop contracts. Such contracts gave a worker a certain amount of time to join a union after being

Members of the Brotherhood of Sleeping Car Porters celebrate the union's thirtieth anniversary. A. Philip Randolph is holding the left edge of the union's banner.

hired. This provision led to the passage of state "right-to-work" laws.

One reason people opposed unions was communism. Many members of the Communist party of the United States joined labor unions in the 1930s. During World War II, the United States and the Soviet Union were allies, so few saw much danger in allowing Communists to enter or even lead labor unions.

At the beginning of the cold war between the United States and the Soviet Union, people began to see the small but influential number of Communists in labor unions as dangerous. What if a Com-

munist union leader called a strike to weaken the United States's economy to bolster the Soviet Union's?

At the CIO convention in 1949, Walter Reuther, president of the United Auto Workers union, led a move to throw out unions led by Communists. The United Electrical, Radio, and Machine Workers union was the first to go. The following year, ten more unions were expelled from the CIO. The expelled unions lost membership and power. Most disappeared. One, the International Longshoremen's and Warehousemen's union, survived for many years.

After World War II, the members of the American Federation of Labor and the Congress of Industrial Organizations realized they had more in common than they had thought. The old rivalry between the two organizations lessened as each came to understand the power organized labor would have if they were united.

George Meany of the AFL and the CIO's Walter Reuther began to talk. They reached an agreement whereby the AFL would not try to steal workers from the CIO and vice versa. It was an important step forward.

In 1953 the two organizations began to work on a constitution to unite them as one group. It was a long, slow process, but by 1955 the two labor organizations were ready to merge. During the first week in December 1955 the AFL and CIO merged into one body—the AFL-CIO.

The American labor movement has faced many challenges and overcome many obstacles. It has had to deal with a sometimes unfriendly government, hostile employers, arguments within itself, and many other problems.

There have been accusations of "un-Americanism" leveled at organized labor. Government investigations have revealed criminal activity in it. There has been violence within it.

Organized labor is an imperfect movement, but it has had some spectacular successes. It has unquestionably raised the standard of living of the average worker and improved the conditions under which all Americans work.

New problems appear every day, among them foreign competition. The unions gained major pay raises for workers, and their members enjoy a high standard of living. But now there are products made around the world that are comparable to, or even better than, those made by American labor. Because many foreign workers earn much less than their American counterparts, prices for their products are cheaper. This is creating a crisis for American companies and American unions.

Union membership has been steadily declining, reducing organized labor's once powerful influence. By 1945, at the end of World War II, 35.5 percent of all workers in the United States belonged to unions. By 1980, when there were twice as many workers eligible for membership as in 1945, only 21.9 percent belonged. Nine years later, only 16.4 percent of U.S. workers were union members. But in the words of one labor historian, "The importance of labor unions in American life cannot be measured by the number of workers who are represented by them." Millions of nonunion workers enjoy the better pay, shorter hours, and safer workplaces that were won by organized labor's long struggle.

The union movement is attempting to find some way to deal with these new problems. It may reach an imperfect solution. But as history shows, it will be a solution aimed at helping its members. As Samuel Gompers said, labor's goals are

To protect the workers in their inalienable rights to a higher and better life; to protect them, not only as equals before the law, but also in their health, their homes, their firesides . . . to overcome and conquer prejudices and antagonism; to secure to them the right to life, and the opportunity to maintain that life; the right to be full sharers in the abundance which is the result of their brain and brawn, and the civilization of which they are the founders and the mainstay. . . . The attainment of these is the glorious mission of the trade unions.

These words are from a speech Gompers made in 1898, thirteen years after the founding of the AFL, but they still ring true today.

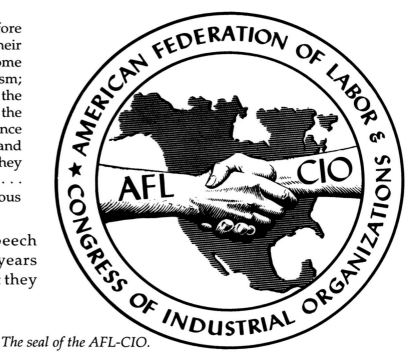

The seal of the AFL-CIO.

Important Dates in American Labor History

1648   Coopers (barrel makers) and Shoemakers guilds founded in Boston; the earliest known unions in North America.

1778   New York City printers strike for a minimum wage.

1792   Shoemakers in Philadelphia start local union.

1794   Typesetters in New York City start local union.

1827   First city central labor organization, the Mechanics Union of Trade Associations, founded in Philadelphia.

1834   First try at establishing a national association of trades: the National Trades Union.

1840   President Martin Van Buren orders ten-hour day for federal workers.

1850   Samuel Gompers born in London.

1852   Typographical Union founded—a national union that is still in existence.

1859   William Sylvis organizes the Iron Molders Union.

1863   President Abraham Lincoln issues the Emancipation Proclamation; all slaves are freed after the Thirteenth Amendment to the Constitution is ratified, creating a large new group of workers. Samuel Gompers arrives in the United States.

1866   National Labor Union started. Its aims were too diverse and the union disappeared after three years.

1867   Shoemakers band together as the Knights of St. Crispin.

1868   Eight-hour day established for federal workers by Congress.

1869   The Knights of Labor begin a history of successes and failures. Although it lasts into the twentieth century, the Knights' influence is small after Haymarket Riot.

Not all union members worked in mills, factories, and mines. The Grange, a farmer's union, was founded in the 1870s; this is one of its early posters.

1877   Major strikes against the Baltimore & Ohio Railroad and the Pennsylvania Railroad lead to the intervention of federal troops.

1879   The Knights of Labor elects Terence Powderly Grand Master.

1881   Federation of Organized Trades and Labor Unions begun; the ancestor of the American Federation of Labor.

1886   Haymarket Square Riot occurs in Chicago. American Federation of Labor (AFL) founded.

1890   United Mine Workers organized. This was *not* a trade union, but an industrial one.

1892   Homestead steel strike in Pennsylvania.

1894   American Railway Union strikes against the Pullman Company; Eugene Debs becomes influential as a result.

1900   Founding of the International Ladies' Garment Workers Union.

1901   Five-month strike against U.S. Steel fails; union weakened.

1902   Hatters' strike in Danbury, Connecticut.

1911   Triangle Shirtwaist Company fire in New York City kills 147 people and reveals terrible working conditions in garment industry.

1913   Encouraged by President Woodrow Wilson, Congress establishes the Department of Labor.

1914   Clayton Anti-Trust Act strengthens unions' position.

1916   Child Labor Law passed by Congress.

1924   Samuel Gompers dies.

1932   Norris-LaGuardia Act passed; establishes the right of unions to organize.

1935   National Labor Relations Act (Wagner Act) passed; guarantees collective bargaining. Committee (later Congress) for Industrial Organization (CIO) formed under the leadership of John L. Lewis.

1937   The United Automobile Workers Union (UAW) stages successful sit-down strikes at General Motors and Chrysler plants. Ten striking steel workers are killed by police in South Chicago, Illinois.

1938   Fair Labor Standards Act passed; establishes the first minimum wage.

1940   John L. Lewis resigns as CIO president.

1947   Taft-Hartley Act passed; limits the power of labor unions.

1949   CIO begins to expel unions controlled by communists.

1955   AFL and CIO merge; George Meany is president and Walter Reuther vice president.

1957   Congress investigates corruption in labor unions.

1972   President Richard Nixon orders ninety-day wage and price freezes to curb inflation; organized labor opposes the measure.

1981   Strike by air-traffic controllers; President Reagan orders them back to work.

1984   The "Ad Hoc Committee for an American Solidarity Movement" is formed; declaring that "American unions are under attack," it seeks to improve the reputation of organized labor.

1989   Minimum wage is scheduled to rise to $4.25 by 1991; it had remained at $3.35 for eight years despite rapid increases in the cost of living.

A woman worker speaks with a member of a union's grievance committee.

INDEX

Page numbers in *italics* indicate illustrations

SUGGESTED READING

Archer, Jules. *Strikes, Bombs and Bullets.* New York: Messner, 1972.

Claypool, Jane. *The Worker in America.* New York: FranklinWatts, 1985.

Dulles, Foster Rhea. *Labor in America.* New York: Crowell, 1955.

Gompers, Samuel. *Seventy Years of Life and Labor.* New York: Dutton, 1957.

Lens, Sidney. *Strikemakers and Strikebreakers.* New York: Lodestar, 1985.

Moran, Frank. *"The Eye That Never Sleeps."* Bloomington: University of Indiana Press, 1982.

Pelling, Henry. *American Labor.* Chicago: University of Chicago Press, 1960.

Voss, Frederick, and James Barber. *We Never Sleep.* Washington, D.C.: Smithsonian Institution Press, 1981.

Weisberger, Bernard A., and the Editors of LIFE. *The Age of Steel and Steam.* New York: Time, Inc., 1964.

Picture Credits

The AFL-CIO: 59.
The Bettmann Archive: 57, 61.
Free Library of Philadelphia: 28.
The Granger Collection: 8, 16, 19, 21, 22, 24-25, 32-33, 39.

Library of Congress: 34, 35, 36, 40, 43, 47, 48, 60.
George Meany Memorial Archives: 6.
New York State Historical Association: 27.
Archives of Labor and Urban Affairs, Wayne State University: 9, 10, 13, 14, 18, 30, 31, 42, 44, 45, 46, 49, 51, 52, 55.

About the Author

Patricia Simonds, a native New Yorker, worked as a researcher and later a magazine editor before she became a middle-school librarian. After many years she escaped the tangled grove of academe and now writes and edits books for middle schoolers.